Dystopia

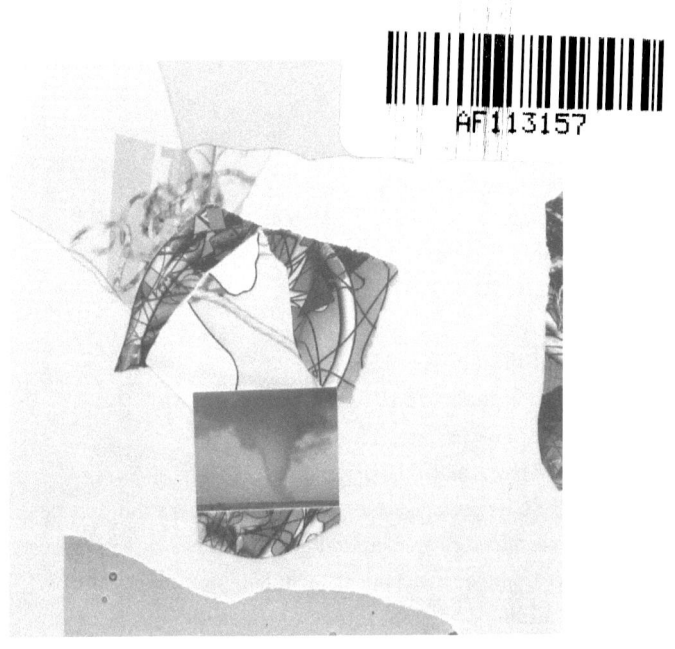

Poems by Steve Gerson

Spartan Press

Spartan Press

Kansas City, Missouri

spartanpress.com

Copyright © Steve Gerson, 2026
First Edition: 1 3 5 7 9 10 8 6 4 2
ISBN: 979-8-89975-022-9
LCCN: 2026934511

Art Editor: Collin Thomas
Author photo: Tom Tarnowski
Cover image: Larry Thomas
Title page image: Larry Thomas
All rights reserved. No part of this publication may be reproduced or transmitted in any form or by any means, electronic or mechanical, including photocopying, recording or by info retrieval system, without prior written permission from the author.

Acknowledgments:

"3 a.m.," *Indolent*

"Heart Disease," *God's Cruel Joke*

"A · ban · don," *In Parentheses*

"OCD again, again, again," *Vermilion*

"Screamscape," *Vermilion*

"Self-Portrait as Hologram," *Panolplyzine*

"Existential Cataract," *Gasconade Review*

"Flayed," *Scapegoat*

"Dementia," *Scapegoat*

"In this time of anxiety," *Scapegoat*

"Self Portrait in Ice," *In Parentheses*

"After Thought," *Coffin Bell*

"Venom," *In Parentheses*

"like snakeskin glistening on the beach," *Contemporary Haibun Online*

"PTSD," *Dillydoun*

"The Price," *WILDSound*

"Submerged under Eclipses," *God's Cruel Joke*

"Hacker's Rap," *WILDSound*

"Word Stumble Fumble," *Quibble*

"The Plaintive Moans of a Dry Man," *Wingless Dreamer*

"A Modern Epistolary," *Bookends*

"Happy Birthday, Dear Gabe," *God's Cruel Joke*

"Terminal," *Contemporary Haibun Online*

"Dregs and Dreams," *CafeLit*

"Pressure," *Vermilion*

"Cage-breaking," *Rainbow Poems*

"Chemotherapy: A Love Story," *The Listening Eye*

"The Mountain Metastasizing," *In Parentheses*

"He Dreamed," *Bear's Paw*

"Eight to Five, Forever?" *CafeLit*

"Teeming Shores: a Triptych," *Palisades*

"Only geese fly straight lines," *Untenured*

"Dinosaur," *CafeLit*

"I Like the Heat," *CafeLit*

"East into the morning sun," *South Platte River Review*

"I've written your name," *MusePie*

"Radiance," *Wingless Dreamer*

"Replete with luminescent artistry, Steve Gerson's latest volume sparkles amid tales of love, loss, desolation, and hope. In crystalline poetry and prose, *Dystopia* captures the present Orwellian state of Amerika ruled by a would-be king. But the sheer beauty of Gerson's verbiage surmounts all, ranging from the love of his life to renderings of tortured relationships, Kafkaesque imaginings, and the fraying of a nation's promises and ideals. Presented by a patriot confounded by his nation's turn, this book is masterful, memorable, and meaningful."

>   -Dr. Robert C. Cottrell, author of the
>   two-volume *Revolution, Counterrevolution,
>   and Assassination.*

"I've followed Steve Gerson's poetry for years. I've seen him tackle disease, culture, politics, life, and much more. I'm struck by this new book as I find it just a bit more aggressive and pessimistic than the previous entries, but for good reason. The United States has entered into unprecedented territory, and this is reflected in the words within this book. Gerson's poems mirror how all of us feel as we slowly descend into *Dystopia*. As a photographer and artist, I am particularly drawn to the use of light and dark to depict moods and emotions. In all the darkness of our daily lives, he sums up our times, our culture, our lives with one simple question: 'Can Light Emerge?'"

>   -Collin Thomas, Media and Marketing Manager

"In these turbulent times, we can find solace in our expressions of thoughts, feelings, emotions, and aggravations. We can use poetry as an outlet for feelings too big to express in simple ways. Steve's poetry gives voice to readers' amorphous ideas and fears. For those who don't have the same ease putting thoughts on paper, Steve's voice expresses things typically too intangible to make solid. Read this and know you're not alone. Even in darkness there is light. While things may seem dire, change is always possible. But, sometimes you just need to yell loud enough for others to hear."

-Stacy Harken, JD, Information Architect/ Technical Writer

"Dr. Gerson has once again stepped further into his poetic genre with his ninth book of poetry. Building on his past successful insights into nature and human experience with shared observations, *Dystopia* takes us to the dark side of human survival and existence in an ambiguous and disconnected society. Like Orwell's 1984, bleakness is pervasive, yet within the poems like 'Existential Cataract' and 'Hacker's Rap,' a connection is created with the reader as an aware human being in a not-so-human world driven by aging cultures and artificial intelligence, all without clear boundaries or meaning, or any sense of value. My favorite selection brings crows out in winter to survive in the dark and cold: 'Self Portrait as February' speaks personally to me. Although perhaps this book could be considered somewhat dark in terms of theme, the depth of human consciousness within each piece certainly makes this collection one of Gerson's best."

-Dr. Bill Lamb, English Professor

Introduction

Come on! I don't know about you, but OMG! I'm bummed. I'm exhausted. I'm stressed. We're a mess. Autocrats rule, oligarchs benefit, liberalism (liberal arts in universities, liberal thought throughout the land) suffers. Remember freedom of speech? And still prices soar, books are banned, wars continue, the greenhouse boils, and the 99.9 percent struggle.

Is there solace? Can we wait this out? Will norms return? Will the center hold?

I have my doubts. This hybrid chapbook of flash, haibun, Fibonacci, interior monologues, experimental works, dreamscapes, surrealism, haiku, and stream of conscience chronicles our challenges, our collective stress.

But, maybe love and hope are always the answer.

Table of Contents:

Prologue

I. The Road Mires in Darkness

The US of Dystopia / 1

3 a.m. / 3

Heart Disease / 4

A · ban · don / 5

To excavate lost thought, / 7

OCD again, again, again / 8

Screamscape / 10

Gone / 12

Self-Portrait as Hologram / 15

Existential Cataract / 17

Flayed / 18

Books and Bridges / 20

In this time of anxiety, / 21

Self Portrait in Ice / 23

After Thought / 25

Venom / 26

A Diary in Delirium / 27

Confessions of a Social Media Misfit / 29

PTSD / 31

The Price / 32

This Year Darkening / 33

Submerged under Eclipses / 34

Things Wrought / 36

Word Stumble Fumble / 37

Hacker's Rap / 38

The Plaintive Moans of a Dry Man / 39

II. Can Light Emerge?

Who Wins? / 43

Golden Age / 44

A Modern Epistolary / 46

Happy Birthday, Dear Gabe / 47

Terminal / 50

Dregs and Dreams / 52

Hopper's Nighthawks,
   the Darkness in Light / 54

Self Portrait as February / 55

Pressure / 56

Cage-breaking / 58

Darkness Lightening / 59

Centerline / 60

Beyond the Horizon, Maybe / 61

Chemotherapy: A Love Story / 63

The Mountain Metastasizing / 64

He Dreamed / 66

Eight to Five, Forever? / 68

Teeming Shores: a Triptych / 70

Only geese fly straight lines / 72
Dinosaur / 73
I Like the Heat / 75
East into the morning sun / 77
darkness the light drinking / 79
I've written your name / 80
Radiance / 82

Birds flew upside down—
distressted symbols in soot-filled air.
On the horizon, clouds piled like question marks.

For Sharon, always

You In All

How to write you paint you sculpt you
script you in song build you as edifice
taste you you are blueberry ripened into
sweetness with tang of complexity not one
note but a symphony of trills that ripple as
arpeggio a house of many rooms waiting
in open doors all glass sun streaming no
hidden corners where dust might linger
a Caravaggio of chiaroscuro with shadows
uplit by an ever present light a Rodin
mother with child the stone softened by
embrace all love songs singing of need
want hope ardor touch I'll write you
sing you sculpt you adore you forever

Prologue

Psalm 23, Product Recall

The constitution was my shepherd. I should not have wanted
(if lawmakers had abided the law rather than fear being primaried).

The constitution now maketh me run from ICE arms:
it deports me over troubled waters.

Its aberration in the small hands of a bloated man
depletes my soul, for he leadeth us in the path of
divisiveness for his ego's sake.

Yea, as I walk through the valley of oligarchy,
I fear evil, his retribution a rod against my back,
his staff of toadies seeking ways to disenfranchise.

He devours my freedoms at the behest of mine enemies:
he batters my head with truncheons, my blood spilling over.

Could goodness and mercy restore our rights?
Surely an enlightened electorate could evict
this false lord from our people's house.

I. The Road Mires in Darkness

The road wends rutted
Sunset sizzles when horizons despair
Our steps hobbled by hope

The US of Dystopia

mouths stopped with ash
burned words bitten tongues
eyes blindfolded with strips
of shredded law ears
cramped with rant
wearing weights melded
from mindlessness
to diminish the workers
stooped over benches
pounding words like
freedom and choice and hope
into sharp edged fractals
to be fed to new recruits
marched into the arena
readying for battle against
new recruits who had been
fed pounded words like
hate and anger and despair
the opposing recruits battling
before the pleasure of a raucous
crowd of loyalists who shouted
banal inanities their mouths
misshapen by intravenously
accepted obedience who happily
wore electronic wristbands
programmed to jolt them with
shocks of acceptance all under
the beaming gaze of leadership

festooned in narcissism the society
worked like a well-oiled chainsaw
a well-oiled wood chipper devouring
Self

3 a.m.

I see evening all day, 3 a.m. every hour,
and the day's night sounds like dissonance,
a dream distorted to blue and black.

In the nightly day, I run fearful streets,
looking back on crows flying crooked
through slanted air, a house with vortex windows,

the door a jagged maw, a dog moaning, its flaming fleas
dancing a derelict jig. Heat sizzles into cold, expiring
on darkness like moonglow behind a constant cloud.

Heart Disease

His heart was like a threadbare shirt
in a thrift store tattered and soiled
often unwanted shelved in dark corners
of his lover's disregard

Or was it him not her his heart marble
petrified wood impenetrable to care so
that affection directed bounced off
with a thud

Her heart was a well seeking water
a planting bed dry from drought so
that buds of desire shriveled into
cursive s's and f's dissatisfied

Or was it her not him her heart a
tentacle probing grasping strangling
suffocating weaponized to defend
and attack

Their hearts diseased ventricles
coiled to thrust not pulse to repel
not embrace together beating in toxic
constriction

A ban don

Noun: My room was dark in abandonment.

Adjective: An abandoned Christmas tree,
hospice-delivered but forgotten,
leaned against a corner void
to my right. No tensile streamers.
No string of colorful lights.
Dry needles littered the floor,
thirsting.

Verb, past tense: Ambient light
like a lost guest seeped in through
the window to my left. A dim glow
had abandoned the wintery gloom,
sun setting behind disturbed
clouds reflecting gray snow.

Noun: I could hear but not see cars
speeding with abandon, their whoosh
the sound of my intubation wheezing,
heading rapidly toward a hazy destination.
Minutes before, my caregiver had read
the chart hanging from my bed like an
amputated foot. "How are you?" he asked,
but his phone interrupted.

Verb, present participle: He held up one finger
in pause, said, "Got to get this. Be back soon,"
before he left the room abandoning me to silence.

Adjective: From my window, I saw a skeletal cell tower, out of service, no reception. An abandoned grocery cart, wheel-deep in snow, sat empty in the cold field, wind whistling through it as a marrowless bone flute to awaken specters.

Noun: I was dark in abandonment.

To excavate lost thought,

I descended into the library's basement, dark, silent, no sounds of shushing librarians, fingers to lips, no murmur of students mouthing sonnets, no skitter of skipping children seeking to find the fate of rabbits in gardens, a girl through the looking glass, hobbits in the shire, only discarded books banned into despair. The tomes lay upon each other as if hiding from air raid sirens blasting red alerts. The books leaned against each other like trees blown apart in volcanic eruptions. Spines broken, the books were dusted in motes settling as lost rainbow gold turning black in soot. Pages were sealed in disuse. No green light shone for Gatsby. Jackie Robinson would not steal homebase. Rosa Parks would never sit in the front of the bus. Huck would not find his territories. No Finch would subdue a mockingbird into justice. The caged bird was mute, in this subterranean land of lost thought.

Syntax silenced,
Thought ground into gruel,
Sentience punished.

OCD again, again, again

2:47 a.m.

I'm watching myself washing my hands, six times, air drying, before trudging slowly to class, as if I'm walking through seaweed-clogged seas, hugging the wall to avoid contact, looking down to avoid contact. Arriving. 1, 2, 3, 4, 5 . . . Putting on my latex gloves. 1, 2, 3, 4, 5 . . . Turning the doorknob. 1, 2, 3 . . . Waiting to a count of 1, 2, 3. Closing the door. Turning the knob . . . 1, 2, 3. Taking off my gloves. Cleaning my glasses, then turning to the wall (counterclockwise only) to check my zipper. Cleaning my glasses (again), then checking my zipper (again). Turning to the class (clockwise only), and saying without looking up, eye contact could lead to interaction, "Good morning, good morning, good morning. How's everyone, how's everyone?" Placing my dry erase markers on the desk, blue then green then red then black. Aligning them exactly 2 inches apart, three inches from the left side of the desk, 4 inches up from the desk bottom. Ready to teach, fearing a student, male, female, non-binary, neurodivergent, whatever, might come to my desk, enter my space, breathe in my clean zone. Uh oh. Here comes one, gender bending, wavering like a hologram. He's, she's, they are explaining why he, she, they haven't turned in the assignment, again, telling me about the latest illness (ADHD, PTSD, PMS-- TMI!), how society is against him, her, them, how their social media sites are slut shaming, outing, doxing, bullying them . . . Oh no! The student is reaching out a hand. Germs, contact, skin, humanity. I try to back away. I try to look down as if focusing on something else. I try to drop my briefcase as a diversion. I scream aloud in my dream, sounding like a whale calf underwater searching for safety. I dive deeper into REM, hoping for nothingness. False alarm, the student is just handing me papers, late assignments, again. "Thanks. Please place them on the table," I mumble, sleep-drooling doubt. I see the papers wriggle, alive with germs, scorching across the desktop. I'll let the papers sit for an hour, a millennium, an eternity through the class to kill most of the germs. When the students leave, I'll put my gloves back on, spray the papers with sanitary cleanser, and then put them in my briefcase. "Good morning, good morning, good morning. How's everyone, how's everyone?" I wipe off the desk with a swipe (4 times, left to right) of sanitary cleanser. I wipe my feverish forehead with the sanitary swipe. I squirt Murine in both eyes twice. I swig, gargle, and spit Clorox. I inject lighter fluid in my veins, again and again and again, until I awake, sweating poison pellets of anxiety.

2:53 a.m.

Screamscape

Can you tell me about your dream?" the VA hospital psychologist asked.

Dream, I thought. Not quite the word I'd use. Dreams always implied wishes and cotton candy and big-ass red Corvettes and Tahiti and tiny umbrellas in coconut drinks and beautiful babes and children flying kites in April and money. I wasn't having dreams.

Each night for the past eight months since out-processing, leaving Afghanistan, shedding the heat like sheep sheared of their winter coats, seeing the sand diminish from the DMZ like time lost, the portholes of my transport plane misting in misery, I landed in nightmare.

Here's what I had earned in my tour of duty: Sergeant's stripes stitched on my sleeves, a purple heart hung around my neck, PTSD pinned to my chest like a service medal, and night terrors buried in my brain like IEDs stuffed inside a dog's carcass.

Each night, I'd hear the howls of shattered bones sprouting from the desert like death totems, see blood dripping from splintered words spoken through mouths of broken teeth, taste the smell of cordite sizzling torrid air, feel my fingernails ripping through hope like skin shredding on concertina, touch shrieks of cluster bombs dappling my conscience like hypodermic needles. And see them, victims of war. The men beside me on dirt trails that wound like intestinal coils through cold mountains. The villagers who saw our presence as ghouls, eating their valleys like flesh.

Each night my head screamed. Each night I turned my sheets into wet gauze, encasing my body in surgical bandages. Each night my eyes blared red like sirens. Each night my blood pulsed through my veins like rotor wash. Each night I woke shouting dead men's names, this my Cocteau Rimbaud screamscape. Each day I feared the next night.

After waiting for a response, the psychologist asked again. "Can you tell me about your dream, Sergeant?"

I reached into my back pocket for a handkerchief, raised it to dab at sweat pocking my forehead like shrapnel, brought the cloth down quickly to wipe away a tear I hoped the doctor had not seen, and said, "No. I can't remember anything."

Gone

The empty chair
at the end of the dock
stared blindly toward the sea
surrounded by clouds
gray as coffin liner cloth.

. . . .

"Joan, when did you lose him?" Sue asked, new to the trailer park, living just two double-wides down from Joan.

When, that's the question, Joan thought. He died exactly 28 days ago, pulmonary infarction the medical chart in the VA hospital said. But he had gone long before that.

Over 700 days before his death, he started leaving. Pieces of him fell away like a worm-holed structure, termite-ridden, leaving trails of sawdust on the floor. The doctor declared early onset dementia.

She lost him when he left behind civility, angering easily at minor infractions.

"Why's this damn chicken so rubbery, girl. Can't you cook no better than this!" he'd scream. "You call this bed making! I've seen tighter corners from my raw recruits," he'd shout in his gruff Army sergeant tone.

She lost him when he lost his way. A reconnaissance specialist in Afghanistan, he always found his target through dead reckoning. But one day, he left their trailer at 11:00 a.m. By 3:00 p.m., she was worried. At 6:00 p.m., she asked her neighbors to help her search. She found him at 8:00 p.m., shivering by the dock.

"Hey Ben. What are you doing? We've looked everywhere."

He turned to her, his eyes vacant, black as undertow, and said, "I went for a walk, somehow ended up here, but I don't know where here is."

She lost him when he lost his memory. Once she went into the den, and he said, "Hello mam, may I help you?" ever the gallant officer but without a hint of recognition. Or she'd enter their kitchen, and he'd look at her with fear, shuddering, "Why are you here? What do you want? Leave or I'll call my wife."

She lost him when he lost his words. He'd try to speak, but his words were like waves rippling toward shore, never reaching land. His thoughts were like a stone thrown into the bay, sinking into silt, creating concentric circles that diminished into emptiness.

She'd lost him before the dementia. He joined the Army two years after their marriage and shipped out for his 12-month tour of duty in Afghanistan. He returned with PTSD, a shrapnel sliver in his conscience, and terrors wrapping him like concertina wire. At night he shouted out dead men's names like bloodied words from a bitten tongue. In the day he narcotized with bottles of Budweiser, French kissing their long necks like a lover.

"Joan. I wondered when you lost him," Sue asked again.

Breaking from her reverie, Joan said, "Last month. We were happily married for two years," not telling Sue that he had been gone much longer.

Self-Portrait as Hologram

Bam. Bam. Bam. Loud knocking on my door.

"Hey, you! Sam. I know you're in there. Open this door, you hear me?"

Half in, half out of my apartment's third floor window, I started to climb onto the fire escape to avoid him, the super, not having paid my rent this month, again, for the fourth time in six months, due to having lost another job, my third in a row, if you force me to be honest.

The latest HR dude said in the exit interview, "You're neither here nor there, are you? More absent than present, more exit than arriving. Just a no-show in general, huh? We feel like we hired a fleshless phantasm, an aura of irrelevancy, an apparition of indecipherable angst, a sort of 3-D person, more spectral interference than substance. When we asked your colleagues about your work ethics, they said, 'Who?' We couldn't find anyone who remembered working with you. All I can say, Sam, is good luck." Then he ushered me to the door.

So here I am, in ether, not in a building, not on the ground, just hovering in midair, this time on a rusted, rickety fire escape barely bolted to my tenement's crumbling, 50's, post-war brick facade. I'm swaying. I'm wavering. Light beams from the surrounding buildings are reflecting through my nothingness.

I'm looking down at the weeds smothering the building's façade. As an expert on imbibable analgesics, you know, booze, I see relief, the glinting telltale signs of broken beer bottles, shards of glass sharp as scalpels honed against the rough edges of my anxiety. "A few stab wounds, a stinging laceration might help. I'd rather be a mess of self-injury than what I am now, a hologram."

Through the open door
Motes drifting in death spirals
The empty room screams

Existential Cataract

I had my eyes checked today.
It seems I've seen life through
cataract lenses all gray

and distracted, my periphery
dim my distance contracted
in shadows with edges myopic.

My soul's a corneal hole distorted
from what's rosy and pure
as if on day one of creation

my DNA missed the memo
about light's expiation
from darkness. So I've stumbled

past colorless mores. I'm all styes
of stigma. What should be black
and white, you see, for those enlightened

has degenerated my cataract
topography. I've become a
fathomless depth of moral opacity.

Flayed

That's me on the table pinioned
by angst, my tendons ripped and tied.
I'm sipping ether narcotized
and looking at an Xray of my evisceration.

I see I think a reflection in the surgery room's
halogen lamp, hot as the eighth circle of hell,
my lies of self, and specters come and go,
clothed in bones.

I know I'm somewhere in the blackness of the room,
my teeth gnashing like a metronome,
my tongue swollen in rant and looking at life
through trifocals smudged in delusion.

I'm dressed in old stanzas from another person's poem,
ill fitting. A Rimbaud tie, the waistcoat Apollinaire,
one sleeve Poe, the other Cocteau. And Duchamp
    shoes worn
on my hands to warm my soullessness.

I look down upon my flayed self to see my heart
tapping like a hammer flailing at nail heads
tap/tap/tap/tap
driven into pine planks.

I bolt upright from the gurney's straps
and roll my sleeves up, my arms tattooed

with liver spots, scrivener's glyphs
demarking my experience without innocence.

And now the end, Byzantium, my hair thin,
my eyes glazed, words on a page through
my fractal trifocals as hazed as worms,
slithering maggots, I'm wriggling on a pin.

Books and Bridges

1. Winter Home

To escape the cold, he lived his winter months in the downtown Unity Street library. During the day, he ambled through the stacks, visiting the warmer climes in the world atlas aisle, 917-919; fishing with Ahab and that old man of the sea, Am Lit, aisle 810; recounting tours of duty with fellow Army vets, Custer in Bio, aisle 921, Patton and Bonaparte in Military Hist, aisle 355. He found these friends through dead reckoning learned in the corps, friends as dependable as due east, west, and south on his military-issue compass. But true north was his nighttime hidey-hole. He'd evade the shushing librarians at lights out, final bell, and bivouac in the fourth-floor men's room, third stall from the left, locking the door, secure in his winter home.

2. Summer Home

In good weather, he lived in the underpass at 12th Street and I-35 highway, sleeping on a scrounged tarp, covered with newspapers reporting problems with the homeless, and bunkered, protected from predators, behind a boma of trash piled around him: a bicycle once red now the color of blood stains, one wheel missing like an amputated leg; plastic bags floating like nightmares from a warzone; a cordless lamp offering no light; empty tins of food having fed someone else; a rocking horse, headless as if guillotined, weeping for a child's lost innocence; and his various battle medals hanging from a rusted, metal Christmas tree like ornaments from a condemned building's white elephant sale ("Cheap! No Value! Given while Serving"). Other unhoused left him alone. He had everything he needed, secure in his summer home.

In this time of anxiety,

I hide. From the fear. My fear of fear.
Fear of touching. All those virus-besieged
canned goods in the grocery stores. I'm
scrubbing my hands with antibacterials.
Wearing two masks. Fear of touching
you, too. Will you respond? In kind?
Will you recoil? As if I'm virus-besieged?

Fear of commitment. To you. To my
current job. Not a career, just a job.
My IDP asks, "What do you want to achieve
this year? In five years?" I might as well
write my plans on sand, on a beach, sea-level-rise
    eroding.
I might as well write my life plans on Snapchat.
Deleted after 30 days if/when unopened.

Fear of failure. Or success. Fear of wars. Even peace
    is frightening,
because then I should be happy, right? Fear of high
    prices. Fear
of forest deforestation and floods and hurricanes and
    polar ice melt
and mortgages and tribal politics and Kardashian
    clickbait and my car
breaking down and a tooth cracking when I have no
    dental coverage
and rogue dogs and road rampages. That's me,

    jumping, like an
emaciated polar bear from shrinking ice floe to
    icebergs calving.

Don't even mention cyberattacks on my already low
credit card rating by Russian hackers demanding
cryptocurrency ransoms. I've never committed
    a crime.
So I fear police will stop me for some minor infraction.
"6:00 pm News Flash: man shot while failing
    to change
lanes correctly. Police report that he wasn't obsequious
when questioned."

So I hide.
With my pulse ratcheting.
Like 7.2 seismic spikes.
Under fault lines.
And I quiver.
With one eye peeking.

Fearfully.

Self Portrait in Ice

The rain snows like frozen pigeons
falling from a gray sky.
Ice sleets the streets in disgust.
I'm slipping on miscommunicated trust.

Why is not the question.
The answer is on my cold skin that shatters
as ice crystals, erupting in fractals that slice.
My conscience is in glacial upheaval.

See the blackening roses latticed with spider webs.
See the ice that coagulates in my veins
and drips slowly from the slash in my side.
See my frozen terror cracking like a winter pond.

I'm as rabbited feet scuttling from red foxes
to leave white prints in the black snow,
glyphics reading like a child's scrawled letters,
screaming.

I'm as a bloodied blue jay skittering across the snow,
scribing dissonant diatribes feathered by broken wings.
My breath steams on a cold windowpane as rivulets
of blood streaming in tears from a swan stranded in a
    frozen lake.

My eyes stare from under the iced eaves
of a farmhouse shrouded in white mists,
my brow the abandoned nest of shrieking starlings,
my tongue the mangled shards of winter wheat moldering.

And I shiver, ice plunged, ice encased like peacocks
    plummeting,
their plumes shredded in angst. And I cry with the creaks
of wooden skiffs trapped in ice floes, drifting, the wood
wailing as limbs torn in a winter storm, wind shearing.

After Thought

after wind shears
after angry sea clouds
serrate like knife edges
after palms shed leaves
in torrents of despair
after winds sting with memory
like shrieking sea birds
after fears lace in seaweed nettles
and strangle
after seashell steps break
into contempt
and blood seeps into sand
after waves spray thought thoughtlessly
like I've thought words onto you
each word a shell sliver under skin
after you asked why
and I answered
with a hurricane's dead eye
after sorrow like rainfall
and skies blackening
I swim toward undertow
tasting salt on my bitten tongue
as waves retreat seaward
in my low tide

Venom

He was coiled.
Others saw passivity,
mistakenly, but behind
his hooded eyes peered
deception. Within his barred
mouth, fangs dripped beads of
venom tearing at my trust.
When he said, "I'm sorry, babe.
She didn't mean anything to me.
It'll never happen again," I felt
the hiss of his tongue flicking
the air for the scent of his next
infidelity.

A Diary in Delirium

1.

I'm eating broken glass,
the shards, words of darkness
like hope, sheared into fractals,
and I'm spitting droplets of blood
onto pages as garbled consonants.

2.

My split lip seethes. My hearing is
plugged with nonsense. My eyes
are cataract, myopic with worms
squirming in predatory journalism
from influencers smogging me in lies.

3.

Why does life provoke with rainbows
after clouds, illusory mirages of
want gratified? Why does the heart
defy the head, all those fissures of cerebral
crenulation mapping lost direction?

4.

I yearn for narcotized thought, to be numbed
in the pitiful prayers of an atheist. I ache in the
aching body of a wracked soul, soulless as a scarecrow
eaten by crows. Shimmering blackness, they peck
at my eyes with bloodied beaks and caw derision.

5.

And this is it? Daily, moment by moment, inundated with shrapnel as in a hell house of mirrors, hallucinatory images of reality fracturing, impaling, derailing, thrashing, and I feel my brain seeping through my ears as sludge to drop as manic motes upon a floor of dust.

Confessions of a Social Media Misfit

"FOMO is no LOL (sad face emoji)," he wrote in his online journal app hoping that everyone would like his secret thoughts. "I mean, I follow her every day, every hour, going sleepless,

Mom yelling 'turn it off!' ignoring Mom, chugging Red Bull with a chaser of Jolt and swigs of Mountain Dew for dessert. I missed studying for my Psych(o) test, again, and sure I tried a bit of playful cyberbullying, but no harm there. She was getting on my nerves, always more pins, more likes, more thumbs up than my feeds, feeding my aggression, I guess. I'm tired, becoming fuzzy-brained staring into this void that pulls me down like an undertow into the third circle of Hell.

Wait. I've got to check an incoming text. Ok, back now. Just my Dad sending me a photo of him and his third wife and their kids (my step sibs, I guess) from their vacation in San Diego.

Wait. She just updated her social photo. Damn! More followers. She's got 7,000+. How's that even possible? Our school only has 1,000 students, and I'm at 56 followers (Wait, what? I'm down to 55 now. Someone just unfriended me!).

Uh oh. She logged off.
Now what can I do? I'm empty, alone in my dark room in the green glare of my monitor surrounded

by Pokemon posters. I'm unplugged from her, stalking, addicted, and mainlining meta air. I can't sleep.

Who else can I troll tonight?"

> *Electrical coils*
> *Plugged into the ethernet*
> *Snakes in the garden*

PTSD

I hear the buzz of starlings swarm
and cloud the sky in blackening drear
their fearful clattering in harm,
their murmurations shriek and warn
my empty house cloaked in fear.

Each day the thousands pale and fail.
They die like shredded shrouds tear
and curtain my mind's wail
while plagues of garbled voices rail
my empty house cloaked in fear.

Wars uncivil, terror flights,
fists uplifting in despair,
the urge to love succumbs to fight
the right with words, the wrong with might,
my empty house cloaked in fear.

It's chattering of starlings crazed.
A man goes down as truncheons rear
in blood and bones and faces dazed.
broken beaks shredding unphased,
my empty house cloaked in fear.

The Price

Off to the left, not fifty meters
from the bunker busting bomb site,
they protruded from the Gaza dust,
tank track treads bisecting them like
scalpel-sliced, surgically impaled remnants.
The arm seemed to be that of a child,
perhaps due to what appeared to be
a cartoon-charactered image still
visible on what might have been a
shirt, but rags rarely tell stories clearly.
The head wears a bloodied cap,
maybe Kippah, maybe Taqiyah,
but religion disappears under
rubbish and wounds take precedence
over Torah or Koran like angry pages torn.
The leg, a stump of a hump of flesh,
torn and raw, red and ragged, toes
blackening, might have been a man's,
but who knows what gender becomes
when bodies are insulted by the cost of war.

This Year Darkening

I feel it, this year, as a bird fleeing
with mottled wings from a songless cage.
This year, I feel it, bone cells dying,
necroptosis serrating to amputate.

I see it, this year, words undulating,
hazed as gnawing worms on a writhing page.
This year, I see it, rough boughs of shaking
trees, limbs bowing from age's pillage.

I hear it, this year, a white wind whining
in moans, groans of life's fading umbrage.
This year, I hear it, a faint song singing
of love loss, of life losing, disengaged.

I know it, my rusting clock unwinding
this year, my darkening shroud awaiting.

Submerged under Eclipses

Drowning in her laptop monitor, streaming Hulu horror shows, she wept dry tears. Her anxiety, red as fear, boxed in her heart racing like rabbits from foxes, each beat a skitter of terror, her chest a constricting cage, her breath heaving for escape. And she scratched welts on her bare arm.

"Why?" she asked, more a shriek than a moan, a groan more than a scream, as if her angst bubbled up from being submerged in sludge, a life trudging through want.

Each day, today, last week, tomorrow, she darkened, the darkness creeping on her skin like cobwebs dreading daylight, filaments fearing a dissembling breeze, like kelp wavering in the doubt of cold currents.

Sometimes her fears unsealed and she saw relief. She breathed breath in ease. And the sun shone, though clouds gathered in the east, a distant thunderhead building with serrated edges.

"Yes, I'd like that," she cooed when asked to meet. "Yes, I can be there at 8:00," she demurred, though 8:00 was late for her needs. "Yes," she said, though she meant "no," her voice muffled as if under waves. "Yes, that's ok, if that's what you'd like," she said, looking for an exit, her eyes darting like bait fish from predators.

But, often, too often, undertows appeared, bruise-colored, blue-black, deep in panic, darkness again, the hole opening to emptiness. And she'd sink, grasping at options that tore her fingernails ragged as hope.

And the day became night, always. And she swallowed eclipses.

Under water, breath burns.
Sight blurs in cataracts.
The Sea's blue blackens in depth.

Things Wrought

Try if you can to see the sky,
blue for those even happy at night,
but plight and strife darken life.
Terrors tame light creating things wrought,

and shall and will become sodden sighs
when realizing that try but cannot denies.
The road seemingly straight dips and dies
descending into troubling things wrought.

Or suffer an esophageal probe
to find the source of your wayward soul.
What lies within the twists and folds,
the mangled morass of things wrought--

skin, breath, psychic mold?
Destructive coughs, destructive thoughts?
You're delving to find the exit toll,
with blighted sight lost in things wrought.

Personal, political, spiritual, climatical
knot in tangles of intestinal coils
that burst like shotgunned crows from flight.
Sun-leaping happy men, their waxed wings
melting, plummet from sky in things wrought.

> *The crow's darkness engulfs.*
> *Its black eyes devour.*
> *Night shudders.*

Word Stumble Fumble

I packed my front yard with signs
telling the world of my neighborhood
exactly how I feel about the day's politics
don't do vote yes no fear the right left
I even strung lights that twinkled flashed
spelling out my voice in dots and dashes
so even low-flying aliens could detect
my opinion and choose to beam me up
or not for further investigation and/or
dissect me inspect me reject me (respect
me?) but it's all so jumbled that I'm
stumbling fumbling like the bumbling
wordsmith that I strive strove to express.
Actually, I think I've knotted myself in
Gordian word mazes, stubbed my toes
on vowels and consonants, rhymed my
reasons senseless, and swallowed my
tied tongue on too many thoughts.
I'm ankle tangled in the jangle of electrical
lines crossing my lawn like tripwires,
and I've fallen into the trap of my words.

Hacker's Rap

Gird your fears stay tuned in
prepare for financial ruin
I'm coming to get your
alphanumeric password
spim spam skim flam
thank you mam
phish spoof splash slash
brute force hash attack
backdoor botnet bottleneck poke
crash crack creep cloak
malware frack adware bleed
money misdeed shattered creed
keylog smog scraper tomb
breached payload logic bomb
social engineered hack slap
hacktivist jab clickjack
fuzz bug infosec
wardriven SQL inject
deep web dark web
hidden web forbidden web
packet racket fake worm
maladjusted toxic squirm
encryption rootkit login smog
Trojan whitelisted spoofing bog
evil twin viral smishing sniff
data meta mega maga rift
crypto doxxing cypher black hat
it's a zero day ransom hijack attack

The Plaintive Moans of a Dry Man
Thou exists on many a thousand grains that issue out of dust
(Measure for Measure, Act 3, Scene 1)

I'm old. I'm dry. The marrow in my bones
moans like Mahler's plaintive flute.
My walk stumbles with brittle hips.
I shuffle in small steps, hesitant to meet
what's cowering beyond the corner
hedge turning brown in a dusty sky.
My eyes see blurred through cataract
haze, words wriggling on pages like
casket worms. Sound comes to me as
crow coughs from a dark mound.

I reach to turn the doorknob with palsied
hands, fingers crooked as question marks.
Why have we surrendered to evil, history
smoldering in charred pages, the predator
teeth of war raking children's innocence?
Why have we stopped our ears with ignorance,
humming banalities that allow tyrants to walk
upright from their coiled nest of serpent sleep?
Why am I shrinking from your touch,
from the sun, seeking shadows?

What slithers from the edge like
an eclipse of fear, darkening our days?
Our crimes hang from wrath-wrought trees
like plums rotting in impudence, the plum pit
stuck in my throat like doubt. All around I see
feathers molting from crows, their black

iridescence shimmering in accusations. All
around I see rose bushes black in decay. All around
I see vanity of vanities, blackening in broken
mirrors, my fingers shredded from glass shards.

And in this depraved month of my dry age,
my dry brain, my dry tongue bleeding on words
as ragged as assonance, gulf winds blowing
warning signs red and black, the spider's web
unraveling as worried syntax, I and you and we
and us are tenants of condemned homes.
We are ghosts of what could have been.
I am lost in time's tumult of broken bones.
I am dust, blown as from a god's hand,
nonchalantly.

II. Can Light Emerge?

A bird flying seeks
escape from a songless cage.
Mottled wings are frayed.

Who Wins?

This country moved against that country,
this region attacked that region,
said the nightly news, but no.
Countries and regions consist of lakes
and streams and mountains and roads
and birdsong. Wars aren't fought
by buildings leveling knockout punches
or flags flying sorties. Wars are fought,
instead, by raw recruits dreaming of a desired
first kiss, who barely know a rifle stock from
general's battleplan, by children scrounging for
turnips amidst TNT, by mothers wailing for their
son's or daughter's or husband's severed arm
lying at their feet like a memory. War isn't
a proclamation delivered thousands of miles
away by a committee of old men. It's the
smudge of dust on a child's face streaked
by tears looking like the clawed talons of a
raptor, deafened ears struck dumb by bomb
bursts, a nose made wretched by the cordite
of gunfire, a soldier's nightmare years later,
awakening at midnight to the howls of bones
screaming, the horror of blood-stained roses
weeping, words seeping from torn mouths with
tongues gnashed by broken teeth, fingernails ripping
fear like concertina wire on scabbed skin, and loss—
homes, hands, hopes shattered as by shrapnel.

A Modern Epistolary

Jane,

I've been thinking of you lately. I'm sorry our relationship ended as it did. We were so sympatico, always in the same orbit, my sun to your moon. Remember when we walked the Plaza that April day? We stopped for ice cream, some of the chocolate dripping down your chin. I wiped it off with my sleeve so your white dress wouldn't smear. Pretty gallant, huh? We laughed about your job as a hairdresser and the weird people you'd meet, that dude with a mohawk and nose rings, the chick with seven colors of hair like a mood ring gone psycho, the grandma with blue hair and perm ringlets so tight her brain was starved for thought. Are you still working there (I can't imagine why)? How's your mom, that old witch? Man, she hated me, though all I ever did was treat her with respect. Anyway, I miss you, hence this text. Yeh, I left suddenly, but you know how my job is—big things to do, important places to see. Do you still have my CDs, especially the Guns and Rose's we both loved. I'll always think of "Sweet Child of Mine" as our song. You take "me away to that special place." I'm going to be in town next week. Want to hook up, Babe?

....

Jim,

Next week, don't call, don't text, don't drop by my house, don't come near me or my friends. In fact, I'd prefer you avoid my zip code. Let me correct several of your misconceptions. First, that April on the Plaza, I told you I didn't want to go, that I had my April hay fever, but you, of course, ignored my wishes. There we were, out in a windstorm, me sneezing, wheezing, coughing, and feeling awful. When you took us into the ice cream place to order, I tried to remind you of my lactose intolerance. You ignored me. And who uses a sleeve to wipe up anything? Were you raised under some bridge by trolls? Oh, my dress was red, not white, BTW. Thanks for remembering. Second, my job. You always put me down for "only" being a stylist. As if your job as a roadie for a garage band was brain surgery, you toting amps, plugging in guitars, picking up the band's trash after a gig at the local dive. I worked hard for my license, and my clients are like family to me. I value the "dude," the "chick," the "grandma." They trust me with their appearances, and I try to meet their expectations with professionalism. Finally, mom died last month after a courageous struggle against leukemia. She was worth about twelve million of you, Jim. Several of my friends and I got together after you left on the band's road trip, one whole state over. We celebrated your absence by drinking watermelon vodka spritzers and burning your damn disks. The Guns and Rose's CD burned into cinders, your sun eclipsed by my moon, especially after I doused it with lighter fluid. I was never your child, your baby girl, your sweetie pie, your pumpkin, your doll. So no, we won't be hooking up. PS—I've blocked you, unpinned you, unfriended you. It's all thumbs down, "Babe."

Golden Age

"How ya doin' bud," Cal asked his bowling partner Jim, Jim's head buried in his Rocket Money budgeting app, the green light from the monitor casting a pall on Jim's ashen face. Jim looked up, his eyes sunken as the hole in his finances, and moaned, "Eggs, $4.95 a dozen. A gallon of milk, $4.25. One gallon of gas $3.15. I take my family, me, Sue, and the twins, to McDonalds, $27 later, I get back into my Ford with 195,000 miles on it belching exhaust fumes, other cars honking at me, shooting me the bird, my kids burying their heads in shame, and I can't buy a new car, not with tariffs ratcheting up the sales price by $8,000. My family has outgrown our two-bedroom cottage that I bought for $125,000 when I was flush with money out of college, just trying to pay off my debts, but now a starter home with four bedrooms costs a million and more, so me and the family are stuck, living on top of each other like crushed cans in a dumpster. Oh yeh, I lost my job last week, governmental cutback, DOGE attack, so the President can have his 'Golden Age of America.' Plus, without an income now, we need Medicaid. That's one, big, beautiful mess. Uh huh, I'm doin' fine, Cal. See you in the unemployment line."

Happy Birthday, Dear Gabe

"Happy birthday, dear Gabe, happy birthday to you!" The hospice staff sang.

"Blow out the candles, Gabe," they all encouraged.

Gabe gummed his jaws a bit, spit out some yellow phlegm, and snorted, "I'd rather piss on them damn candles, if I could. But, I can't stand up to do so, plus I ain't got no piss in me no more."

"Say my man, how's it feel to be 196 years old? I can't imagine anything cooler than eternal life," said Doug, his head keeper.

Gabe scratched his bald head and grumbled, "Well, let's see. My ma and pa died 'bout 8 generations ago. I saw all 27 of my kids go before me, plus of course six wives. Then I buried 84 grandkids, 316 great grand babies, 997 great great grandkids. You see my point, dumbass? I got more death in me than a convention of morticians. I seen more caskets than whole wars ever buried. I done wept enough tears to fill this here city's water system. Go ahead. Drill into me like a basin. I'll fill you up with tears.

But hey. It ain't all bad," Gabe said with a wheeze as he sucked on an unfiltered Pall Mall. "I also served in 4 wars, had a hundred or more jobs, doing everything from mayor of this here city, plus its fire chief, a principal of the high school, janitor, farmer, rodeo calf roper, car thief, pimp, and drug dealer. You can do bunches of shit in 196 years.

And all because of that damned drink I slurped way back when. 'Try this,' the carnival barker said. 'It's an anti-aging serum, chocked full of good stuff. It'll add maybe 10 years to your life.'

Well, I was coming off my second heart surgery and thought, 'Hell yes. We got debt. My family needs my earning power. So I swigged it down. No tellin' what was in that swill. Probably turpentine, some rattlesnake venom, a pint of rye whiskey, and maybe ground up pig's testicles.

I never imagined that those 10 years would last 140 more. And look at me now. I'm 4'2" from my original 6'1". I weigh 79 pounds. My ears are longer than my hair. I wear quadrifocals that give me at best 20/70 vision. In other words, I'm looking at you, Doug, but all I see is a shadow behind a cloud as if inside an aquarium filled with sludge. And I hurt all over. My arthritis has arthritis. I'm bone on bone. I can't walk no more. My legs are as brittle as dry wheat shafts. I've broken every bone in my body dozens of times, just from coughing. I've got so many wrinkles that I look like a sequoia and 'bout near as old as one.

But I tell you, Doug, this ain't goin' on much longer. Uh uh, no way. You know those pain pills you give me? I've been hiding 'em," Gabe said with a wink. Yep, I'm getting out of this purgatory. I'm

tired of falling asleep hoping to never see another
dawn, but come sunrise, there it is again. Life."
And Gabe spit more phlegm, black as anger this
time, black as hope eaten by a murder of crows.

"One day soon, I'll have enough pills to kill all
my lives, and you ain't going to find where I hid
'em. So, to answer your question, how's eternity
feel? It feels like having a root canal every day for
a century, like seeing man's stupidity rerun on a
loop in slow motion every second, like eating razor
blades for breakfast, lunch, and supper, with snacks
of African killer bees, washed down with battery
acid, like losing love and your heart shredded by
zombie fangs dipped in botulism.

You want that? Eternal life?"

Doug thought a bit, rubbed his jaw, and then
replied, "Oh yeah, give me that drink. All I see
is an eternity of beer, watching sports games, and
dating killer chicks."

Gabe closed his eyes. Another rerun on a loop in
slow motion.

Terminal

Look it up. Webster's defines it as "end of the line, Bud. You're on your way out." My doctors agree. Lung cancer, terminal. And I feel it. I'm breathing like a 1957 Ford truck with a bad carburetor, huffing, puffing, wheezing. Every bone in my body rattles. My tires are flat, and moss is cementing me to the asphalt. My side panels aren't just rusting. They're eaten through as if my innards are corrosive. That's not even the worst news. No food. I get no steak and potatoes on my way out. I get no lemon meringue pie or even sweet tea. Nope. Instead, I get a plastic tube through my nose, pumping something yellowish into me, like Satan's sulfur. It reeks of seaweed flavored with acetone saturated in the chemical waste from a water purification plant peppered with hand sanitizer and a whiff of putrefied compost.

But I've put one over on them. My friend, the only one who visits me in my hospice cell, sneaks in booze. I'd say, "rot gut," but that would be a pun, given my body's status. So when the nurses are off doing their nightly record keeping and the place is morgue quiet, usually around 2:47 p.m., I creep out of bed, dragging my various wires, tubes, and hanging bags, my accoutrement, as my long-gone, French-teacher wife would say, her nose all primrose and lavender, twist open the metal cap from my secreted bottle of Johnny Red, take a tasty slurp, and feel the burn from the third circle of Hell. And I say, "Come and get me, you damned Harpies," fists clenched.

Waves crashing
A voided message
In an empty bottle

Dregs and Dreams

The neon glare through the bug-splattered window suggested life, but I was trapped inside the diner by lies and lassitude, nursing a cheap cup of bad coffee more dregs than dreams.

Hunched, alone, I could see my reflection refracted in the coffee's sheen swirling like an oil slick dragging me down in an undertow. I looked up. The neon blinked in intermittent gasps.

"Where to go next?" "What to do next?" I asked myself.

I'd made mistakes before. Many. Often. I'd said, "I'll try harder next time" and failed. I'd said, "I won't do that again" and failed. I was recycling bad decisions, stuck in a constant pattern like a sewing machine, needle going up and down, up and down, the stitch always the same, the design never changing. Repeat. Repeat. Repeat.

All she'd asked for was hope and not even much of that, maybe a teaspoon rather than a ladle, just a taste, not even three courses.

But here I was, looking at my distorted reflection. And the coffee was becoming cold as loss.

The diner's waitress stopped by my table, a carafe half filled with bottom-of-the-pot coffee, and nodded at me, suggesting a refill.

"Hit me again," I said.

Hopper's Nighthawks, the Darkness in Light

While others converse
she contemplating her cuticles her role in red
as the soda jerk absorbs obliging noblesse
the worldly insights of her companion
nightly light shining aslant on their interface
crossroads meeting coincidence
the man apart chiaroscuro turns inward
to question darkness

Self Portrait as February

February is insecure.
It teeters on fewer days,
even when more days are added,
as if always deficient.

February is mired in grayness,
the dolorous days of winter,
but midway through, it aspires,
sending love missives written candy.

While crows cloud its skies in blackness,
occasional robins, as if lost in seasonal
shifts, skip in russet and blue.
White mounds of snow chill.

But buds ready for spring's ascension.
I'm as February. I am this month of
Iago and Caliban, Shylock and Malvolio,
distant and detached, neither of nor with.

Crows peck ignobly on worm rot to find sustenance.

Pressure

633 nautical miles, north by northwest of Anchorage,
he died, his crabber capsized by 20-foot sea swells,
the wave crests a crowd of terror swamping his
ice-encased ship sinking into a vortex of undertow,
bow broken, crosstree snapped, outriggers wailing
in siren moans. A distress buoy blinked red in the
black night.

Eighteen hours later, 633 nautical miles, south by
southeast of the Bering Strait, the missing ship
was reported when radar reckonings showed a void
in the ocean when VHF wireless attempts to
rouse a response heard only static, the hiss of loss.

She learned from sea widows used to fear and
foreboding, women who wore the sea's darkness
like a shroud. They soothed her in words she didn't
hear. "It's all right. It's OK. The sea gives to us, and
sometimes it takes. We live the rhythm of the waves."
They comforted her in utterances that groaned as
ice floes clogging sea lanes. All she heard through
the fog of their commiserations was his words.

"Just this last run, babe. If we get a catch, that'll give
us money for a down payment, maybe even a truck.
Then I'll stop. No more high sea's risks in high winds
and bad times. We'll marry and the skies will calm,"
as he ran his fingers through his hair, coiled as a ship's
tangled lines.

Mascara tears running down her cheeks like exclamation points, she went to her bedroom and saw it, her wedding dress, laid out, ready for him.

"Let it go, hon," her dad said. "He's gone, like yesterdays scratched off the calendar. But you can still have a tomorrow. Let it go."

She picked it up, toted the wedding dress heavy in cost, and hung it in the back corner of her closet, the dress's white already turning leaden as grief.

Fog shrouded waves
Crest in cascading fear.
The land awaits light.

Cage-breaking

Yes, like the blown-bird thrown against the gale,
I in my ground-down landscape, earth-footing
dwell, both we cumbered in life-quest lumbering
against what impedes, the seagull's breeze, my dust swale.

The gull above sees sea-ray sun and strives as I
landbound, sand-bound to reach cloudless skies;
we sigh-sing in gawping cries to sail, tearing
our tethers, the gull's feathers rending,

my hope from earth-footed toe-drag risen.
And with a gust the gull blue-soars aloft,
its keening calmed, cloud storms diminishing,

and with the bird-soar, gull-glide in my vision,
I too step from my land-drudge and soul-waft,
the bird and I from earth and sky rainbow flying.

Darkness Lightening

tired   tired of the darkness
dry kindling   dead leaf fall
the dark stinging my skin
with viral spores

parched in the dry night
my throat clogged   with clods of rant
shrouding my voice
muffled

stumbling   through this darkness
bruised on clickbait brambles   pursued by
shrieking tweets
stepping on stones
seeking water to soothe my thirst

seeking light   there
there in my path concentric circles of light rainbowing
I see as if a pail dew-fed
to quench to swab my eyes my throat

flash bang gassed   a sip to cleanse
my labored breathing   and hungering

I cup my hands as in prayer and
kneel to drink

Centerline

I was walking the yellow centerline, dissecting Main Street, downtown Houston, rush hour traffic pooling to my left and right, headlights streaming toward me in horror, horns blaring behind me, warning. "Stupid kid! Get the hell outta the street, dumbass!" I grabbed your hand as we kept walking north to south, people shooting us the bird. "Why are we doing this?" you asked, your hand clammy, August in Houston. The street was hot, smelling of melted tar.

Your eyes were wild, twitching anxiously. Your blue dress was beginning to stick to your skin, the dress turning dark with sweat, clinging to your body. You were beautiful in the chiaroscuro of headlights and shadows.

I didn't know, not really, so I said, amid the shriek of horns and profanities, "I don't want to be fear. I don't have courage to love. I want to find a centerline, but what seems straight keeps twisting," and I held your hand more tightly.

Adrift, winds stilled.
A boat swirls in eddies
To avoid the undertow.

Beyond the Horizon, Maybe

An Ekphrastic based on Andrew Wyeth's "Christina's World"

Her arms bent like brackets to support other's will, never her own. Her back bowed into an S, supine, struggling. Her body was smothered by the land as if kudzu vines strangled her. It was noon on the farm, and the sun cast shadows on her body like bones picked clean by turkey vultures.

"Hand me that saw, Christina, won't you?" George asked, demanded more like it. "You better milk that dang cow, Chris. Can't you hear it bellowing, it's udders about to burst?" he said, but what he was thinking, she assumed, was at least little Joe can get his milk from the cow, since you went dry as a leaky well long time past. "Hey girl, I'm going into town this afternoon. Got some business to tend to. I need you to pick cotton while I'm gone. It ain't gonna pick itself. I know it shreds your hands like a thresher. Maybe you ought to put on my work gloves, you think?"

Going into town for business. Not hardly, she thought. He'll stop by McWard's tavern to sip on cheap, watered down 3-2 beer. He'll lose money at pool, my money mostly, the cash I earned by canning summer corn and squash. He'll spend time with her, that Delilah, with her henna-red hair, her lips like just picked beets, her body all curves. Not like mine, flat as a plowed field, planed straight as raw wood. Then he'll come home, stinking of beer, smelling of her.

Christina, weighed down by clouds, wore a dress once pink, now washed as colorless as amoebic platelets. She looked to her right toward the eastern edge of their sharecropped property, toward their farmhouse. It slumped into the ground, grayed by withering winds. To her left, toward the western boundary, was their barn, stranded like a lost calf. Between the two structures was a thin line, dissecting the land from the high sky like skin sliced by a well-honed sodbuster knife.

"Beyond here is a horizon," she thought, "maybe."

Chemotherapy: A Love Story

"I'm unravelling, John," she said. "I feel like a skein, spinning, splitting, thinning, like a tattered web, windblown and shredded. Insects are feasting on my dreams. A cicada is derisively trumpeting in my rib cage. Bees burble in my veins like kerosene boiling, the chemo drip as insistent as day-long 3:00 am nightmares," she said as she tugged on a pink scarf, pale as hope, covering her remaining hair, a fringe of her diminished past.

"What can I do, Babe?" I winced, powerless against the pain shadowing her like an eclipse.

I reached for her hand, the one not infused, the one not punctured by multiple needle marks.

"Look at me," she moaned. "I'm a tapestry of stitches and seams. My skin is pixilated, a pentimento of blotches. How can you love this?" She ran her hand over her body like a painter trying to whitewash a flawed drawing.

I'd never loved her more. She was not a web of mist but tensile, tenacious, not a thin line sketching a portrait of possibilities, but a canvas gouged by fingernails, grasping at life.

A tree lightning struck
Marred, scarred.
Roots seek sustenance.

The Mountain Metastasizing

1.
The light in the east rained fire and fear,
that *annus horribilis*, pelting us in a deluge
of disease. We trudged as under a dragon's
wings, its teeth bared, eyes yellow,
along a road winding toward
a mountain's dark shadow.
2.
A dark mountain spewed fear
like bats and ravens
erupting from caverns, each day
a stalactite dagger in our chests,
x-rays webbing spider tracks,
neuron snakes, synapses frayed
as if chewed by orcs in steel traps.
3.
Not even orcs in steel traps,
they fearfully shrieking
as infusion weeping,
could deter you, you cloaked
in courage red as the dream
of blooms in spring. Like an umbrella
opening, you shunned our doom,
4.
we doomed to flow in eddies,
sludge muddied, our turbidity
of terror. You called after us
as shepherd to sheep, saying,

*"The dark mountain
is not encased in fire. The light
that rains in the east is dawn."*

He Dreamed

He dismounted from his Ford Desperado, 6.7
L power stroke, v8 turbo, 330 horsepower truck,
mud flaps splattered from weekend off-roading,
boots and Lee jeans muddied as a Pollack drip
painting, held up by a belt and huge rodeo buckle
purchased on sale at JC Penney, wearing his second
cleanest dirty chambray shirt and a free gimme
ball cap with an AAA trucking company logo, and
swaggered like a cowboy toward the Quik Trip for
his morning usual, a large, double whip, pumpkin
spice macchiato.

Walking with a loping gait, bowlegged as a barrel,
he dreamed of bronc busting, which he'd never
done. He dreamed of riding lead drover on a cattle
drive in the open range, which he'd never seen
from his third-floor apartment in a suburb outside
Chicago. He dreamed of freedom, which he'd never
experienced as an insurance salesman.

Fully caffeinated, he readied himself for the
boredom of his day. He was scheduled to meet an
elderly couple to sell them life insurance for their
final ten years of life, boat insurance to a 20-year
old man who had no money to buy a boat, and
long-term care insurance to a young couple who
would need long-term care in about 55 years.

But on his drive to the clients' homes, after he changed
clothes to Gap chinos and a polo, he dreamed. Of
blue skies and wide horizons. Lowing cattle. Black

coffee cooked in a kettle over a campfire. A lariat looping over the horns of a stampeding cow. Maybe sonofabitch cowboy stew, made of some beef and lots of offal and marrow guts. But he settled for lunch in his truck, a bologna and American cheese sandwich on white bread.

His afternoon was the same, one routine sales call after another. One doorbell rung after another. One pitiful attempt after another to convince people to buy what they shouldn't or couldn't.

And in between each call, he dreamed. Of a time when land wasn't fenced by barbed wire. Or even by suburban picket fences. When wildflowers grew wild rather than in window planters. When the nearest neighbor might have been 20 miles away, not 20 feet down the adjoining apartment hallway.

His day finally over, he drove to the Quik Trip again, still bowlegged but more browbeaten in his gait. He pushed open the store door, said "Howdy" to the beleaguered teenager behind the counter, and pushed the coffee machine button for his usual. While checking out to pay for his coffee, he said, "Hey pardner, give me a tin of Red Man chewing tobacco."

As he left the store, he pulled a packet of chew, placed it between his back teeth and jaw, let the juices run, then spit a stream of stain onto the sidewalk, dreaming of doing the same thing from a saddle astride a gelding roan on a prairie, somewhere, anywhere, just not here.

67

Eight to Five, Forever?

Eight to five. Every day. Five days a week. Four weeks a month. Eleven and three-quarter months a year, with one vacation week, unhappily given by my boss. Eight to five, over and over, again and again, stamping metal into food cans for beans and beer, punching holes into metal for pull tabs, the machinery pounding out a symphony of cicada misery until my ears ring like sirens wailing. And my hands burned from hot metal, cut from jagged edges, scarred like a roadmap through the Black Rock Desert of Nevada, land serrated by wind, sun, and despair.

"I can't take it no more, Lucille. This job, this city, this damned life we're living. It's pressed holes in me. I'm lattice work more than man. I'm a sieve. I can't hold a thought with all the noise in my head. I can't hold you with my hands a mess of mangled meat. Come on babe. What you think? We got to get out of here."

Lucille looked at him in the mirror as she ran a comb through her blonde hair, once burnished as fire-forged gold, now limp and pale as butterweed. She saw him reversed, beaten and bowed, the man she had married three years before, he a stud football player on their high school team, she a wielder of flags and pompoms on the cheer squad. She saw in the mirror their squat camper the color of smoke, a dried flower arrangement thirsting for water, a cracked vase bleeding hopelessly onto their Formica countertop, dishes crusty with last night's meal. And a distant light in the window, draped with moth-holed curtains.

She had finished her eight to five shift at the diner, five days a week, four weeks a month, twelve months a year, with no vacation time allowed, her hands burned from carrying three hot plates on her arms, piled with other people's food, while she and Bob ate rice and potatoes and catsup for their vegetable. Her hands red as denial from washing the diner's dishes, her dreams of a future draining down the diner's sink.

She got up from the dressing table, a six" x two" plank of wood swaying on two cinder blocks scrounged from the neighbor's yard, turned to him, placed her hands on his shoulders, and said, "Yes, Bob, let's go. Now's the time."

They threw their clothes into four grocery store bags, picked up their runt dog, and ran to their Ford truck, giggling like children released from school once term was over.

"Where to, babe?" Bob asked.

"Anywhere without clocks," Lucille said.

Teeming Shores: a Triptych

1. What it must

What it must have felt like to land on our shores a dark sea behind them dark clouds of oppression dissipating like a swarm of bees the hissing becoming silent and now just open skies a land waiting to be tilled my grandparents arriving with an alien language of consonants and only hope filling their baggage now reoccurring daily at our borders new Americans wanting to quench their thirst and breathe air without bombs with the unlimited opportunities of limitless horizons what if must feel like

2. A hint of

She left the boat from Haiti sailing on a 20-foot skiff to Jamaica sea-washed salt-sodden with a Coke bottle of fresh water and cooked cornmeal wrapped in plantain leaves hunger as constant as fear she and 22 others barefoot ragged Levis she and her infant daughter tied to her bosom as tightly as a dream and landed in Port Maria darkness becoming dawn wading through the Caribbean onto wet sand her toes digging into a hint of freedom soon

3. Camino Real

Roberto y Isa walked weary through saguaro thorns past coyote screams and dry gulch bones broken dreams of hope scorched in heated air casting mirages on the sand of freedom sought like water in empty canteens

toward the Camino Real a royal road over a wall of
anger a shout of wrath shredding like concertina wire
into Eagle Pass and there on new land saw a future that
opened like air intake on breath-wary lungs

Only geese fly straight lines

The wheel ruts scribed the prairie snow like meridians on traveler's maps, pathways evolving from now to next, lines curving in impromptu plans.

"Where to?" he asked, eyeing the sky as if clouds told tales with trusting advice.

"Try right," she answered. "I always veer toward the shadows," earth askew, trees shedding leaves in winter chill, branches bending above the pond, western shorelines pushed randomly by contrary winds.

"You think it's there?" he asked again.

She breathed in deeply, held a sigh like a wish, then weaving her arm in his, said, "Let's try."

Dinosaur

Sitting on his front porch facing west, he watched his pumpjack struggling, a riderless rocking horse, thrusting like a jilted lover into the earth, hoping for a strike, retracting, hopeless, the well returning dust.

His family had drilled for oil since 1920, the crude barely needed coaxing, ready to bubble up or burst through the derrick like a caged beast. But the well had dried.

He tried fracking to fracture the shale, witching the underground aquifer to loosen the gold, a drone with geothermal compass to ferret his fortune. All failed. Shamans from the Indian reservation asked spirits for guidance. He and his wife Marge even sought help the old-fashioned way, praying in their Pentecostal church, knees at pew, pleading.

"Oh Lord, feed our land. Provide our needs. Use your mighty hands to raise the dead, oil that you have hidden in the reticent crevices of our dry soil. Let the black spew forth, we pray."

Still the earth withheld the oil deposited 300 million years earlier in the Permian Basin outside Odessa, Texas, where pterodactyls and velociraptors compacted into dead organisms. So he sat, drinking his 4th Bud Light, draining it, crushing the can, and tossing it into his yard to gather with earlier crushed cans, littering like metallic weeds.

US 87 highway ran north to south a mile from his ranch. He could see cars on the overpass, driving somewhere, anywhere, away from the land. The sun was setting. He sat in the lengthening shadow of the highway's darkening underpass, the earth stealing light.

I Like the Heat

It's hot. My asphalt street is melting like the La Brea Tar Pits. But I'm the dinosaur this time. My bones are old. I'm petrified, not just from ossification but from fear.

How did the dinosaurs feel, I wonder, when faced with extinction?

Did they huddle together for strength? I could do that, I guess, gather my ilk of old buddies, swig bottles of beer with chasers of whiskey to narcotize my demise. "Hey, old man, pass me a Bud. I need numbing."

Did the stegosaurus bow in wingless bird prayer with the velociraptors, forgiving each other's willingness to maim or be maimed? I could do that, I guess, gather my old coworkers, all of whom I fought with for survival against deadlines and corporate expectations, and pray for collaboration. "No, Carl, let's share. You take the PGM account this time. I'll get the next one."

Come on! Who am I kidding? I might be a dinosaur, but I have no desire to pray or gather, to placate or befriend. Kumbaya my ass. The hell with them all. I'll stick to my predatory ways.

I'm going to eat up as much life as I can before the sun broils me to death in its moral equivalent of climate change.

Here's the plan. I'll sharpen my blades, honing my rough edges against life. No more dull me.

"Sir, there's only one chocolate chip cookie left. Could my little girl have it?"

"Nope. I'm on my way out, I mean really on my way out, and I'm taking this cookie with me. She can get one some other time."

"Could you hold the door for me, please? I've got my hands full."

"Nope. My hands are full too, with life's challenges."

Get the picture?

The dinosaurs caved to an asteroid attack, so we're told. They froze, starved, or were blown apart by explosions, debris, and tree shrapnel.

I might be facing extinction, the dying of the light, but I'm not going to cower in a corner, sniveling, shivering, shaking in despair, pleading, "Woe is me," like Hezekiah begging for more years to his life (Look it up. 2 Kings 20:1-11).

I've got both fists raised. I'm ready for a fight. I like the heat.

East into the Morning Sun

"I've had enough, Mom," Rosie said, slumping, running her fingers through her mess of red curls, her hair as tangled as a tumbleweed thrown up against a barbed wire fence along the roads outside Amarillo. "I've had enough of truckers pinching my butt, enough of customers at the Stop and Go drooling over my breasts, thanks to the too tight cashier's blouse my boss insists we wear. I've had enough of college students after a late night drunk leering after me as I walk by, muttering just loud enough to hear 'I want some of that' or 'Yum, that's what I call grade A beef.' I've had enough of the poor pay and late hours, and I'm really tired of having so little time with my babies. By the time I pick them up from daycare, usually late, all I can do is feed them, bathe them, and tuck them in. That ain't quality mothering."

"So what are you going to do?" Rosie's mom asked.

"I'm getting out of here."

"And what's going to change? You'll still be you wherever you go," her mom said, always the defeatist.

"New day, new way, Mom. I'm not going to keep hitting rinse and recycle, like on our old washing machine. I'm going to embrace whatever waits for me."

With that, Rosie kissed her mom, belted the kids into the back seat of her Honda Civic, 257,000 miles, held together with duct tape and hope, and drove east from Amarillo to Dallas, into the morning sun.

The sun broke
like an epiphany.
A path shone.

darkness the light drinking

behind the light where darkness lurks
beyond the storm cloud's angry murk
where rain pelts the sodden dirt
the black maw is screaming hurt

and I am struck as raw tinder
by viral screams my skin tender
to the touch in decaying winter's
leaf fall and fear and frailty enter

my swollen psyche my tongue burned
but from the dark reflection turns
as sky above pooling water spurns
the grief and spots the sun's churn

and there is hope from this anger
respite from this danger
of governments and sickness strangling
I see light as if a thirst answered

I've written your name

I
have
written
your name on
lines of text threading
silk like gold on spun tapestries

twirling to earth in arabesques
like spring leaves that swirl
your name penned
my hand
in
yours

I
have
written
your name on
air through breezing trees
blown in gentle sighs to embrace

the sky in pastel hues of love
rainbowed arcs that paint
your name on
gray clouds
shone
blue

I
have
written
your name in
rhyming tunes that pulse
with heat and punctuating heart

starbursts beyond infinity
I've written your name
breathed your scent
held you
in
love

Radiance

Paper and pen could not suffice.
Ink and intention would not merit,
quill on parchment or chisel on stone,
this world's implements too lacking
in intensity for your perfection.

Only heavenly script could draft
your name on constellations,
the letters drawn in stardust,
my fingers weaving a trail
through Cassiopeia and Aries,

sighing the syntax
of Andromeda and Cygnus,
your name shining in the night,
backlit by moonglow and love,
the skies treasuring each syllable,

and yet, the starshine
paling against your presence,
weakened in your illumination,
for how could sun, moon, and stars
compete with your radiance?

Dr. Steven M. Gerson, Professor Emeritus, Johnson County Community College, Overland Park, KS, was named 2003-2004 Kansas Professor of the Year, chosen by the Carnegie Foundation. He is the co-author, along with his wife Sharon Gerson, of 13 college-level textbooks and the author of eight poetry chapbooks: *Once Planed Straight: Poetry of the Prairies; Viral: Love and Losses in the Time of Insanity; The 13th Floor: Step into Anxiety; And the Land Dreams Darkly; Who Am I Today* (Spartan Press-KC); *There is a Season; Have Not (Online Journal of Arts and Letters)*; and *What Is Isn't*. He has published over 400 poems in many journals and is honored to have been named a finalist three times for the North Dakota State University Press Poetry of the Plains and Prairies award. Steve is most proud of his 55 year marriage to Sharon, for whom all his love poems are written, his wonderful family of Stacy, Stefani, Rob, Bobby, and for the joy of spending time with his three grandchildren: Sophia, Samantha, and Jacob. These people are the poetry of Steve's life.

This project was made possible, in part, by generous support from the Osage Arts Community.

Osage Arts Community provides temporary time, space and support for the creation of new artistic works in a retreat format, serving creative people of all kinds — visual artists, composers, poets, fiction and nonfiction writers. Located on a 152-acre farm in an isolated rural mountainside setting in Central Missouri and bordered by ¾ of a mile of the Gasconade River, OAC provides residencies to those working alone, as well as welcoming collaborative teams, offering living space and workspace in a country environment to emerging and mid-career artists. For more information, visit us at www.osageac.org

www.ingramcontent.com/pod-product-compliance
Lightning Source LLC
LaVergne TN
LVHW041617070526
838199LV00052B/3184